When Shhh is Not Enough

Anne Borrowdale
and
Barbara Wynn

First published in Great Britain in 2013 by
Ashton Pickering Publications
44 Hollow Way Cowley Oxford OX4 2NH

Reprinted 2014
This edition published in 2015

Printed by Inky Little Fingers
Unit A3 Churcham Business Park
Churcham
Gloucestershire
GL2 8AX
www.inkylittlefingers.co.uk

PREFACE TO THE 2015 EDITION

This edition includes minor updates reflecting changes to JCQ rules and the exam system, and practice in exam centres. Sections on Safeguarding and Equal Opportunities are now in Chapter Nine (renamed "Outside the Exam Room") along with a new section on Exams and Social Media.

PREFACE

We originally wrote this book to accompany the training sessions Exam Team Development run for exam invigilators. As so many people found it useful, and there's nothing quite like it on the market, we decided to make it more widely available.

While there are many different kinds of exam centres, this book is specifically for external invigilators in schools or colleges who have to manage student behaviour as well as supervising all the other aspects of an exam. Most schools and colleges in the UK will run some or all of their exams according to the regulations set out in the Joint Council for Qualifications *Instructions for Conducting Examinations*, known as the ICE booklet. [See the Glossary at the end for which awarding organisations this covers.] We try to reflect common, general exam regulations, while noting where JCQ and other awarding bodies have different rules. Your exam centre will train you on the specific rules governing the exams you invigilate.

Disclaimer: While we strive to keep our advice consistent with exam regulations and educational good practice, the guidance given in this book is the personal opinion of the authors, and is followed at your own risk. Invigilators and exam officers must always check and follow the exact regulations of the relevant awarding organisations for their centre, and implement their centre's policies.

Our thanks go to the many invigilators and exam officers – and Andrea Harman in particular – who have shared their experiences and good practice with us, and to Johnny Stormonth-Darling for his cartoons.

Anne Borrowdale and Barbara Wynn   Oxford 2013

TABLE OF CONTENTS

A Tale of Two Invigilators

Ryan strolls into the exam hall with a swagger and a smile. He's capable of at least a C grade if he works, but is easily distracted.

Casually kicking his mate as he passes, he laughs, 'Mind your feet!'

'SILENCE!' yells the invigilator at the front of the hall. 'You come in here in SILENCE!'

'I only –'

'Quiet. DON'T answer me back. Now SIT DOWN!'

Ryan sits, smirking at his mates to save face.

'Ryan! Face the front! I will not tolerate any messing about. If I have to speak to you one more time, you're OUT.' Turning to a colleague, the invigilator mutters, 'What a waste of space. They should take him out and shoot him.'

The exam starts. Ryan opens his paper. He's hyped up, and can't understand the first question. He looks round at his mate.

The invigilator strides to Ryan's desk. 'I warned you …' she hisses, pointing a finger. She remains by the desk, glaring.

Ryan rolls his eyes, drops his head to the desk and goes to sleep. He'll fail the exam, but at this moment, he doesn't care.

But what if a different invigilator is in charge?

'Mind your feet!' Ryan laughs as he kicks his mate's chair.

The invigilator catches his eye. She raises her eyebrows, makes a shhh gesture, smiles, then looks away. You know you need to come in here in silence, is the message, I expect you to do as I say, but I'm on your side.

Ryan sits and completes the front of his paper, ready to work. The first question baffles him, and he looks round at his mate.

Again, the invigilator catches his eye. Knowing Ryan is easily distracted, she gestures to him to face the front and again she looks away, to avoid engaging with him. She keeps an eye on him from a distance, so he'll focus on his paper, not on her. Ryan looks at the first question again, and finds that, actually, he does have an answer.

The invigilator continues to monitor him from a distance, and remind him with gestures if his behaviour slips. When he finishes early and keeps looking round, she approaches him and whispers,

'Ryan, I can see you've finished, but you need to sit in silence facing the front right to the end. Thank you.'

Ryan sighs, but he does as he's told.

Calm invigilating can't guarantee Ryan a C, but at least he's been given a chance, and no other candidate has been disturbed.

CHAPTER ONE

Introduction

Invigilating exams sounds like a peaceful, easy job. You sit at the front of a large room reading your book while the students get on with their work. That's certainly the popular view of the invigilator's role. The reality, as you quickly discover, can be somewhat different: two hours on your feet watching 100 teenagers you might never have seen before, many of whom would rather not be there. A minefield of rules and regulations to learn and apply. Fellow invigilators may all have different approaches. And being an invigilator requires you to be vigilant, so you have to give your full attention to the task and say goodbye to that book!

It turns out that invigilating exams is more than just a casual job. You are supervising the end process of years of education. Your response, as we show with Ryan's story, can make all the difference between students having a good exam experience or a bad one.

External invigilators

After a change to their pay and conditions in 2005, UK teachers were no longer routinely required to invigilate external exams. Instead, schools and colleges began to use external invigilators. This seems to have worked well, leaving teachers free to teach, while the exam team could focus on the smooth and efficient running of exams. Although that situation may change, with more teachers invigilating in future, external invigilators are still likely to be used.

As invigilators, you bring a variety of skills to the role, based on past experience and personality. Some of you are particularly good on the admin side, some naturally observant, some relate easily to teenagers. We've met many invigilators who are excellent golfers, though we're not quite sure how that transfers to the exam hall!

From the administrator's point of view, running exams is a very structured process. There are clear, logical steps to take involving planning and preparation before the exam, conducting the exam, and post-assessment, which should ensure that all the regulations are kept, and the process runs smoothly. Indeed, everything would run like clockwork, exam teams sometimes joke, if only there were no students involved! But students come with their own concerns and queries and don't always behave to order.

External invigilators who are responsible for creating the right atmosphere in the exam hall for students to give of their best, may never have worked in schools or with young people before. And while all staff are responsible for managing behaviour, invigilators face the added challenge of doing it in silence. This requires a special set of skills in behaviour management which invigilators need to develop alongside their knowledge and experience of exam processes and regulations.

Maintaining order

In our experience, most young people do take their exams seriously. But some students do have challenging behaviour, and unfortunately, if this is not managed effectively, the situation can escalate. The consequences spread far beyond the individual who misbehaves. Disruption spreads, and other students get distracted, both by the behaviour and by invigilators dealing with it. If students are removed from the exam hall early, someone will have to be found to supervise them. The well-behaved students won't be happy because they've been disturbed. Subject teachers won't be happy, since they'll get judged on the results of that disturbed exam. Where reports have to be written for the relevant awarding body, information passed to teachers, and letters sent to parents, this takes up time and energy for the exam officer and other centre staff at a time when they are already stretched.

If exams are regularly disrupted, the reputation of the school or college can suffer, with fewer high-flying students wanting to sit exams there. Even more seriously, a school or college which is constantly reporting malpractice, or requesting special consideration for pupils affected by bad behaviour in exams, is likely to come under close scrutiny by the awarding body or JCQ. It could even lose its accreditation as an exam centre.

The move towards linear exams, where students sit one final exam at the end of two years rather than sitting exams in stages, has consequences for invigilation. On the positive side, fewer modules and tiers could make managing exam timings, papers and paperwork less complicated. However, candidates may be more stressed when everything rides on end-of-year exams, and some may struggle in longer and more challenging exams. It is therefore even more important that invigilators manage stressed and/or disruptive candidates effectively.

That's why skills in behaviour management are so important. While you might not have a choice about *whether* to apply exam regulations, you do have a choice over *how* to apply them. Tried and tested methods which good teachers use to maintain order in the classroom can really help invigilators to defuse problems before trouble spreads. Yes, a lot of it is common sense, for example, speaking with a smile rather than stern finger-wagging. But there are also skills which can be developed.

Tips and techniques

When Shhh Is Not Enough offers various tips and techniques to help you manage candidates in the exam hall. As well as advice on how to deal with misbehaviour using our "Ladder of Intervention", we look at developing good relationships with students generally, reducing the stresses on them, and dealing with large groups. We've included stories of successes, and some failures. If you let us know your stories, concerns and tips, we may include those in future editions.

Because schools and colleges are different and invigilators have their different skills, some of the ideas will be more relevant to you than others. So think of it as a toolkit from which you can select, rather than an instruction manual. If you are a qualified teacher, these ideas will no doubt be familiar to you, but we hope you'll find it useful to think about how they apply in the exam hall. Your experience can be invaluable in building an excellent exam team.

Teamwork

Teamwork is vital to the smooth running of exams. It's what ensures that all the paperwork is spot on, that students are properly supervised at all times, and that exam rules are applied consistently and fairly. Your centre may well appoint one or more senior or lead invigilators - as is recommended in the ICE booklet - who can take charge and make appropriate decisions within the exam room. The senior invigilator should keep the invigilation team informed, and keep communication flowing about decisions and incidents. But everyone in the team has a role here.

As we'll say later, it helps if invigilators feel valued members of the school or college team, working within the same policies and ethos. Yet invigilators can feel they're in an awkward position at times. You're part of the institution, and paid by it, but your role is to maintain the integrity of the exam system and report any suspected or proven malpractice by those in the institution. Doing your job well by noticing and reporting malpractice won't necessarily make you popular if it affects the results of an A* student, for example. But if you don't, you put at risk not only your own integrity but the integrity of your exam centre, and in the last resort, this could result in the centre having its accreditation to run exams withdrawn. (The JCQ website has further information, see Glossary p.73.) So it is very much in everyone's interests to work together to reduce or prevent malpractice occurring in the first place.

While there's no substitute for training and practising on the job alongside the rest of your exam team, this booklet can provide you with some useful approaches. We hope it will help you to be more confident, to have more positive relationships with students, to work better as a team, and to enjoy the role. And as a result, the students you invigilate will be enabled to do their best in their exams.

CHAPTER TWO

Before the Exam

Depending on how your exam officer organises things, you may or may not have a large role in setting up the exam hall. Information about this is clearly set out in the ICE booklet or in the specific rules relevant to your examination system, and you will also cover it in your in-house training. We're not going to repeat all the rules and regulations in those documents, but rather we will focus on the things which support you in your dealings with candidates.

Things the exam centre can do

When we ask exam teams what their school or college could do to make their job easier, we get some real cries from the heart. Here are some things centres do which help invigilators to manage behaviour:

~ Providing good rooms for exams, with adequate heating and ventilation, and space not just for desks but for invigilators to spread out papers and equipment, and to move around the room without disturbance.

~ Preventing unnecessary noise. Students who find concentration hard at the best of times get very fidgety when things are going on outside. So while no one expects the whole community to take a vow of silence when exams are on, it does help if students (and staff!) are kept from chatting or playing football outside exam rooms, and the grass-mowing gets left for later.

~ Briefing the students regularly about what's expected of them in exams, so they know how to behave and what equipment is needed if they have to provide their own. Some centres text candidates or use social media to send reminders. It's harder to maintain a calm exam hall when invigilators are rushing around giving out equipment.

~ Introducing the invigilation team to the students during an exam assembly and including them on staff lists or photo lists. This helps to establish that invigilators are in a partnership with the school or college and a critical part of exam success, as well as reinforcing invigilators' authority.

~ Ensuring staff are on hand to get students into the exam venue in an orderly and disciplined manner. Having a member of senior management present during this process helps set expectations for good behaviour during the exam. In some centres, staff will be required to be present to verify students' identity.

~ Communicating the school or college's ethos and behaviour policy. Invigilators who notice a student barely attempting an exam paper or being disruptive can wonder why that student was even entered for the exam. They may be tempted to get the student removed from the exam room as quickly as possible. Understanding that the school or college wants to give every candidate a chance, and that schools are required to enter a high percentage of their students for certain exams, can encourage invigilators to manage difficult candidates better. Where invigilators understand the centre's behaviour policy, they can give students a consistent message about behaviour and its consequences, and know that reports and concerns from the exam hall will be followed up.

We had a student who was a real pain in exams - disruptive, sullen, rude, and always in trouble. Our hearts sank when we saw her name on the seating plan. But at the end of Year 11, she approached an invigilator and asked if she could sit at the back for her GCSEs because she knew she'd act up if she sat in her usual place near her friends and fellow trouble-makers.

We didn't feel much like showing her favours, but gave her a chance. She sat at the back, worked hard at all her exams, and achieved the C grades she wanted. It was very gratifying, and a reminder that even the most difficult young people care and can change.

~ Treating invigilators as part of the school or college community. While invigilating is a casual job, invigilators who make a long-term commitment and get to know the students add a great deal of value to the role. Briefing exam teams generally about news and events helps give a different perspective on students. Invigilators often mention that if they've had a brief, friendly exchange with a student about something outside of the exam hall, it makes it much easier to deal with them during the exam. Briefing about students who need special consideration for such things as illness or bereavement helps invigilators to be supportive - though still under exam conditions, of course.

~ Sharing exam results with invigilators, to help them see the end point of all those hours of work and to give useful feedback for the future. Did the invigilator's quiet word with a student help them settle enough to get their expected grade? Did the classroom noise next door during that A level actually affect results?

You'll probably have other things you could add to this list of what exam centres can do. How much influence the exam officer has on these will vary from centre to centre, but invigilators can do some things for themselves, such as being more involved in their school or college.

Things the exam office can do

Obviously, a well-organised exam office makes the job of invigilation that much easier. But smooth processes also help invigilators manage candidates. Here are six key things which your exam office may well do already, which should help with your task:

~ Preparing early, so that papers, equipment, and exam venues are ready to go on the day. We know exam officers are generally very good on this, even though external pressures and the sheer volume of exams can make it difficult. But when everything is in place in good time, it frees invigilators to supervise properly rather than having to rush round locating papers, desks, whiteboard markers, etc. Students then enter a calm exam hall rather than a crisis centre.

~ Appointing a senior invigilator to whom some of the above tasks can be delegated. As well as assisting in the exam office, this experienced invigilator can be a point of reference in the exam hall.

~ Providing advance information to invigilators about the exams. In addition to knowing what the subject is and how long the exam lasts, it helps invigilators to prepare better if they know how many students are involved and whether any have extra time.

~ Providing enough invigilators, particularly at the start and end of exams and where behaviour is an issue. We do recognise the budgetary pressures on exam officers, but managing behaviour is much easier if there are extra invigilators on hand. Even with perfect preparation, an unexpected query may mean an invigilator has to leave the hall, which leaves the team one short. When invigilators are concentrating on tasks such as taking the register, giving out equipment (if required), or attending to student queries, they aren't watching candidates. They may miss an urgent request for help, and even normally well-behaved students can start communicating if they can see no one's watching.

~ Making it easy for invigilators to identify students. Accurately completed registers and seating plans are compulsory, and there will probably be labels or cards on desks. Having extra copies of seating plans available will help invigilators to identify that candidate six rows back who looks distressed or keeps turning round. Or your centre may have its own way of helping you quickly identify who is in the exam room.

~ Anticipating possible trouble. For example, rearrange normal seating plans if two potentially difficult students will be sitting next to each other. Bring in an extra, experienced invigilator, for exams with potentially challenging students. Or, if behaviour is a real issue in the centre, the headteacher can authorise a member of teaching staff to be present in the exam room purely to maintain and enforce discipline. In that case, both invigilators and staff member need to be very clear about what they can and cannot do and say.

Things the invigilator can do

Managing behaviour is partly about having a calm, confident, authoritative presence in the exam hall. There are some things invigilators can do to help create this presence (even if they aren't necessarily feeling it!) Many of these points are obvious, but we think they're worth noting. You may want to add your own ideas to the list:

~ Know the regulations. Read the ICE booklet or your specific regulations before each exam season to remind yourself of the rules and to see what's changed.

~ Arrive in plenty of time, so you're focused and calm.

~ Ideally your exam officer will have provided you with advance information about the exam you are invigilating, so check you know what and where it is, how many students you'll be invigilating, and the total time you will be on duty. If it is in an unfamiliar venue, make sure you know where the fire exits, first aid room and nearest toilets are. Check you can open windows and adjust heating or ventilation if needed. You don't want to become a distraction to candidates while you wrestle with a sticking window, for example.

~ Look the part. Dress professionally, for example by wearing a jacket. Pockets are useful for carrying spare equipment, or your own notebook and pen. Having layers helps, whether the exam room is cold or overheated. Though avoid flowing clothes which have a tendency to sweep papers off desks as you pass. Remember shoes need to be comfortable enough to stand for long periods, and quiet. Students justifiably complain about the distracting 'clack clack' of heels as invigilators patrol the aisles.

~ If you need glasses for reading or distance, make sure you have them with you. You'll both need to see across a large exam room, and read the small print on registers. If you have hearing issues, come equipped to hear student whispers.

~ Think about what you eat and drink before invigilating. The students will be told they'll concentrate better if they have breakfast and bring a bottle of water - and it's true for invigilators too. You'll want to avoid the kind of lunch which makes you sleepy, and if you bring in sweets or a snack bar to keep you going during a long exam, plan ahead so you can get at them silently and discreetly. However, check what your exam officer allows, as some limit invigilators to nothing but water.

~ Be willing to learn. If you make a mistake, be prepared to admit it and learn from it. Talk to your exam officer and fellow invigilators about how to do better next time.

~ Make sure your mobile phone is silenced, or preferably off (and on mute, so there's no sound if you do have to turn it on). All those warnings to students about phones will be undermined if yours goes off. Some exam officers will ask you to hand in your phone before invigilating, and will provide an exam phone or two-way radio for summoning help from the exam room. If you are required to use your own phone to summon help, have the contact number in it ready for emergencies. If you have been provided with the centre's mobile phone to use in an emergency, make sure you're familiar with it.

~ Be aware of your attitude towards young people, and how your previous experience of education or your practice as a parent can affect your expectations. Teenagers mature at different rates, and some do behave badly. If you can concentrate on the best way of helping them to behave well, rather than giving in to annoyance when they're being difficult, you're likely to find it easier to invigilate them. It is surprisingly easy to be judgemental and to escalate situations by being confrontational. A motherly (or fatherly) invigilator may be over-helpful and find it hard to apply rules. But as an invigilator, you need to focus not on how you feel about whether something is right or wrong, but on how to create the best exam experience for the students in front of you, within current rules. Be vigilant, not a vigilante.

~ While knowing what particular students, year groups or classes are like can be very valuable in anticipating potential problems, be careful not to give in to negative stereotypes. "Oh no, it's Media Studies!" or "Foundation tier students always misbehave" can be a self-fulfilling prophecy.

~ As we suggest in a previous section, take an interest in the school or college community, and do what you can to build good relationships with students and staff. Pass on positive comments about students when an exam goes well.

Things students want from invigilators

Finally, it's worth thinking about what students want from their invigilators. Here are some of the things they say:

~ Keep awake and alert, so you notice quickly when we put a hand up.

~ Don't stand near us whispering, it's very distracting.

~ Don't breathe all over us with your minty breath, or stand behind us crunching your Werthers Originals.

~ Deal with trouble-makers sooner rather than later.

~ Don't yell at us, or make all of us suffer when a few idiots misbehave. Deal with them without disturbing us.

~ Smile!

Question on survey: "What didn't you like about the exams?"

Student response: "The invigilator stood next to me and Breathed."

CHAPTER THREE

Getting them in, Settling them down

For convenience, we look at preparation, starting, running, and ending exams as if they're a neat linear process. Of course a lot of the time, they're all happening at once: you're collecting one lot of papers and giving out another, while simultaneously keeping up with student hands going up for another sheet of paper. However, we'll stick to looking at all these elements under separate headings, again from the particular perspective of managing candidates.

The point when students start filing into the exam hall is probably the time the invigilator's heart beats fastest. Have all the practical preparations been done right – enough desks, correct papers ready, etc.? Will you have a hall of model students or will there be individuals who are difficult to manage?

Keeping things calm

Staff will almost certainly supervise students up to the point they enter the exam hall, especially for GCSEs and large exams. Senior management may authorise extra staff to be present in the exam hall to help as students come in, although this may not always be possible. However, there are strict rules about who can be present in the exam room and what they can and can't do, and staff must recognise this and respect the authority of the invigilation team. As we've said, if teachers have quietened students before sending them in, this will make the invigilators' task of creating a calm atmosphere much easier. But it can be a challenge managing a large group of perhaps 200 teenagers, where the first students are at their desks for a long time while the hall fills up. (Pray that Aaron Aachen is a model student rather than a "character"!)

There's a balance to be struck here. On the one hand, students need to know that they have to obey exam conditions. If invigilators turn a blind eye to chatting before the exam starts, it sends all the wrong messages. On the other hand, many students will be nervous. Boisterous behaviour, irritability, or sullenness may be symptoms of this just as much as a chewed lip and a worried expression. Smiling, and using a low, quiet voice to give reminders about not talking, will help to settle students much better than jumping on them. You may need to use one of the low intervention approaches listed in Chapter 5, such as addressing the group by name with a confident, "Year Ten!" (as appropriate).

The ICE booklet recommends that question papers are placed face-up on desks before candidates enter the room, so that invigilators can focus on supervising candidates as they come in. You will need to be extra vigilant to ensure that no one touches their paper until instructed to do so. And of course papers must never be left unattended.

Phones, bags and watches

Your exam centre will have its own systems for dealing securely with students' phones and bags before an exam. Smart watches and any other "technological/web-enabled sources of information" will also need removing. It's not directly a behaviour issue, although students need to feel their belongings are secure, so they don't risk keeping phones etc. on their person. In some circumstances, students get asked to leave bags at the back of the exam room. It is best to avoid this if possible. As well as the danger of a phone going off in a bag – and trying to find which bag among a heap of 20 is buzzing loudly is far from easy – it may encourage students to feel more casual about the exam. Instead of walking in with nothing but a pencil case, they're tossing bags and coats at the back as if they were in a classroom. If students are sometimes allowed to leave a bag at the back, they might try it on at other times. There are also issues when students come to collect their things – see Chapter 6.

I was on phones duty, scanning the pockets of trousers as students passed through the door into the exam. I spotted a suspicious shape and called the young man back:
'Could I have your phone please?'
 He produced it and gave it to me, then said with a smile,
"But it's all right for me to have it, I'm a teacher!"

Dealing with requests

Having enough invigilators/exams office staff on hand to deal with problems or queries at the start is really helpful in maintaining the right atmosphere. It helps to have planned in advance who will stand where, with some invigilators remaining at the front, while others deal with questions. Some centres pre-allocate invigilators to a specific row of desks in the exam hall, to deal with any issues which arise in that section. This can be useful especially in larger exams. If a seating plan has been displayed on the wall outside, students should know where they're sitting. Of course some of them won't look and others will forget. So it's a good idea to have one invigilator by the door, with a copy of the seating plan, to deal with all seating queries, rather than several invigilators being occupied finding out the information.

If the centre is willing to provide equipment for students who have forgotten it, it's useful for invigilators to carry a few black pens etc. in their pockets to hand out if asked. At the start of a large exam, it may be better to allocate one or two invigilators to give out equipment, so that the others can give their full attention to maintaining exam conditions. Some centres provide several small baskets of equipment around the exam hall, or invigilators take a basket with them when responding to a student with a hand up.

If students are proving difficult to settle, it might be sensible to say you'll deal with a request after the exam starts. For example, fixing a wobbly desk, or finding out a candidate number, could be done quietly while the student is reading through the question paper. But don't forget!

Start promptly

While starting exams usually falls to the exam officer or a senior invigilator, newer invigilators may quickly find themselves having to do it on their own, especially if they're alone in a small exam. You will find an approved form of words in the ICE booklet, or your awarding body or centre may have its own version. Some centres make an audio recording to play before each exam. We believe that varying the wording slightly, using eye-contact and personalising the words to the group, encourages students to listen. But do keep it short; students don't want long spiels when they're all keyed up to start the exam.

It's important to start the exam promptly even if an individual student has a problem or someone is late. It's both unfair on the prompt students, and liable to make them restless, if they're kept waiting. Where a student has a query which can't be dealt with immediately - for example, if you need confirmation from a teacher that a candidate can change from a Foundation to a Higher paper - ask them to wait quietly while you start the exam, and then deal with them. Always reassure them that they will get the full time for the exam.

Occasionally a student will arrive for an exam, but their name is not on the register. Ideally, you don't let them start the exam until you've checked with the exam officer or appropriate teacher that they should be sitting it. Again, ask them to wait quietly, and reassure them that they'll get the full time. However, if this will take time to resolve, it is not only hard on that student, but a distraction for everyone else. It is not maladministration to allow a candidate who is not on the register to sit an exam, provided that their name is added to the register and the exam officer creates a late entry.

Colleges and schools don't usually wait for latecomers once the scheduled start time has been reached. If there are several of them, you might decide to bring them in as group rather than individually. Try to run through the appropriate exam briefing before they come in. Hopefully there will be guidelines on this, but the lead invigilator in the room may be best-placed to judge which option is least distracting. In this case, as with anything out of the ordinary in the exam room, make sure that an accurate record is made of what has happened and what action has been taken. Your exam officer will have given you instructions on completing the correct paperwork, and it makes their lives a great deal easier if you get this right.

When there's a problem

If there's a serious problem such as a lack of papers or wrong papers, invigilators should maintain calm and not scare the students. Rather than specifying the problem, it may be better to say "There'll be a short delay for administrative reasons". Candidates can get restless when they're waiting a long time for an exam to begin. You could use the time to run through a few of the exam regulations which don't get recited before every exam. For example, a reminder about doing all rough work in the answer book, or keeping papers flat on the desk, or explaining what "no communicating" actually means. Always reassure candidates that they will get the full time for the exam once it starts, and that the awarding body will be informed there was a problem. We give some tips for handling large groups in Chapter 6.

Sont les réponses sur le plafond?

I was invigilating a French exam in the French classroom. All the French posters had been removed from the walls, but halfway through the exam, my eyes drifted upwards and I saw there were lots of posters in French attached to the ceiling. I realised that climbing on tables to remove them would be extremely distracting, not to say risky. None of the students had noticed them, and in any case they were very basic French which was unlikely to help. So I let it go, keeping my fingers crossed that an inspector didn't turn up and look up!

It may be necessary to let an exam go ahead even if something is wrong. It shouldn't happen, but life being imperfect, sometimes this is the lesser of two evils. The alternative is a delay, which can penalise students who are anxiously waiting to get going, and a late afternoon exam can disrupt travelling home at the end of the school day. Ideally, you will correct any non-regulation situation quickly, but it may not be possible. The exam officer will give guidance on this, but running the exam under less than perfect conditions is likely to be better than abandoning it. However, make sure you keep a record of what has happened.

The desk check

You will be interacting with students as you look for, and remove, unauthorised items, and it's a chance to be polite and friendly and help them to settle down. Centres vary as to where and how they collect unauthorised items from students, so this may happen at the door, or after candidates are seated. In some centres, students bring nothing but themselves into exams, as all equipment is already provided on desks. Even so, it is worth telling students each time to check their pockets, and to hand in any forbidden items they may have brought into the room.

You might find it useful to carry a few envelopes with you for students to put unauthorised material inside, with their name on, to be held at the front of the room. Making sure that anything handed in is labelled and looked after securely encourages students to keep the rules, and ensures they're not distracted by worry about their possessions. If you remind students to put all the items they need for the exam on their desk - including water bottles and any medication they require - they will have no reason to get anything from their pockets during the exam. That avoids them doing something which can look suspicious and result in an invigilator disturbing them.

Ideally invigilators will do a desk sweep as students are being seated. If you can spot such things as a phone, smart watch, or notes written on someone's hand before the exam starts, it saves a lot of problems later. However, sometimes other demands on invigilators – such as having to give out equipment – means that this can't be done properly until after the exam begins. You will in any case be quietly patrolling the aisles to keep any eye on students, since invigilators are required to move around the exam hall at frequent intervals. Gliding rather than stomping will help you not to distract candidates from their work.

If you spot an unauthorised item after the start of the exam, deal with it as previously described, but also record the time at which you removed it. If possible, tell a fellow invigilator so there is corroboration if a formal malpractice report has to be made. Occasionally, a student wants to argue, but your aim will be to keep things low key, using the sort of techniques we outline in Chapter 5.

Despite any warnings which have been given, you may still observe a suspicious shape in a pocket as you patrol. Usually students respond to a polite request to know what it is. If you find it's a perfectly clean (and blank) tissue or even just a fold of material, you can say a quiet "Thank you, sorry for disturbing you" and move on. If you're really not sure if there's something in a pocket, it's best to wait until the end of the exam before you ask. You don't want to upset a student unnecessarily if your suspicions are false, but do make sure you ask before they leave the exam room. If you do this with a smile and a brief explanation of why you're asking, innocent students are unlikely to mind.

If the student in question has behaviour issues and is something of a powder-keg, you might want to wait until the end of the exam to speak to them, rather than risk causing disruption. Or you could ask a senior invigilator or the exam officer to approach them if the matter has to be dealt with immediately. However, if you have decided to wait to the end of the exam, do let your fellow invigilators know, in case they decide to intervene in the meantime.

Although there are rarely behaviour issues during the first minutes of an exam, there could be queries or equipment failures, and it is vital that at least one invigilator is watching the room closely all the time. Other invigilators will need to complete registers, update seating plans if any candidates have been moved, record absences and notify the appropriate person so that absentees can be chased if necessary. In a large exam, the exam officer or senior invigilator will allocate these tasks. If you are on your own, you will have been given instructions on what to do about registers and absentees.

CHAPTER FOUR

On the Road

So the paperwork's done, everything is in order, and the students have their heads down, working hard. It's tempting to breathe a sigh of relief and switch off. But the invigilator is not like the car passenger who can gaze out of the window or drift off. Rather, you're like the driver who has to keep their whole attention on the job. Some exams are like motoring on an empty road: there's nothing going on but you still need to stay alert in case a hand goes up. At the other extreme are exams which feel like negotiating a complicated junction in the rush hour, when you need eyes in the back of your head. Like the best drivers, a good invigilator is very aware of what's happening around them, anticipates trouble, avoids getting into difficult situations, and interacts calmly with others. As with driving, concentrating for long periods is tiring. A short break every two hours isn't a bad idea, if possible. Sadly, unlike drivers, invigilators can't listen to music!

Practical tasks

Invigilators will have a number of practical things to do during exams, such as:

~ starting and finishing exams

~ keeping the notice board up to date with exams, timings etc.

~ completing registers

~ providing equipment, extra paper, tissues etc. if needed

~ collecting and handing out papers

~ setting up the next exam

The challenge is to do these things while also supervising students, and without distracting them. It's easy for an invigilator who has had nothing to do for an hour to jump at collecting and sorting papers, without realising how much noise it makes for candidates who are still working. Tearing registers apart and sealing up envelopes can also sound loud in a quiet hall. It's worth asking: does this need to be done now? Does it need to be done in here? And if the answer to both is yes, to be very careful that you're not disturbing students. Avoiding distraction is especially important if you're with students who are easily unsettled. The calmer you can keep things, the more likely they are to keep working at their papers.

Toilet breaks and tissue breaks

Exam centres have different policies about toilet breaks. Some ban them, at least in shorter exams. Some have a rule that no toilet breaks are allowed in the first or last 20 or 30 minutes of the exam. Awarding organisations are likely to have their own rules too, principally that invigilators should not leave the exam room if that reduces their number below the required level. However, if a student rushes out of the exam room feeling ill, you may need to follow them even if that leaves the exam room temporarily one short – as long as you are not the sole invigilator, of course.

It's a good idea for the exam team to discuss their "toilet break" strategy beforehand, since taking students out can create problems. You may have to summon help so as not to leave the hall short of the regulation ratio of invigilators. Some exams need more than the required ratio, and it makes things difficult if an invigilator is out of the room temporarily. And it can add to the complications if your centre or the awarding body require the invigilator supervising the toilet break to be the same sex. Also, it is disruptive having students go in and out, even if they do it very quietly – and some of them can't seem to help clattering chairs and treading heavily. Plus, some students are asking for breaks because they're bored or because they want a chance to grin at their friends on the way out.

Whatever the centre policy, no one wants to refuse a truly desperate student, and exam nerves do affect one's bladder - or worse! If you do make an exception on these grounds, let your fellow invigilators know why. A student may complain if they were refused a toilet break, but see their neighbour get taken out. In such cases, remind the student it is a general rule, but that invigilator will have had a special reason to break it for that student. If you've refused a toilet break because of a lack of invigilators, don't forget to offer it if an extra invigilator returns or you are able to get assistance. It's all part of treating students with respect in anticipation that they will behave maturely.

Just occasionally, if you have a student who is misbehaving, it can be a good idea to offer them a toilet break in order to have a quiet word about their behaviour. If you do this, make sure you record it, or tell your fellow invigilators what's been said. It's generally a good idea to record who takes toilet breaks, as a pattern might indicate cheating - see below.

It's not uncommon for students to ask to leave the exam room to clear their nose or cough. Similar judgement is required as to which is the least disruptive - taking them out, or having a nose blown loudly and creating lots of laughter at or with the student concerned. With winter colds and summer hay fever, this can be a real issue. A constantly sniffing student may be more irritating to the invigilator than to other candidates, but you will need to intervene if you see others are being disturbed. You can try patrolling with a box of tissues, or quietly asking if they would like a tissue, though while one student finds it helpful, another might be offended or think you're patronising them. Knowing your students helps here.

Help!

As well as asking for equipment etc., students may have queries about something on the paper, or ask you for help. There are strict rules about helping, and what to do if there is a genuine problem on the exam paper. JCQ instructions are that, if an erratum notice has not been issued, candidates should be told to "answer the question as printed". In rare cases where the problem is that the question does not make sense as printed, this will not be possible. But in any case, you will need to refer any potential mistakes on the question paper to your exam officer. The key thing from the candidate management point of view is that invigilators interact politely and calmly with them in these circumstances, and keep it brief so as not to distract others.

In most cases, the student will have a simple question to which you have one of two answers. Either say, "All the instructions are on your paper", and direct them to the front cover of the paper if appropriate, or say, "I'm sorry, I'm not allowed to help you." If the student persists, take a moment to check you really have understood what they are saying, before repeating your answer and moving on. If it's a legitimate question, but you're not sure of the answer, say, "I'll check and get back to you." You can take the question to your senior invigilator, quickly check the ICE booklet, or contact your exam officer if it is still unclear. But do avoid the "invigilator huddle", where all the invigilators get involved in examining a problem, and no one is watching students.

It's quite common for students to make a mistake on the paper and to be unsure how to correct this. For example, they've written an answer in the wrong place, or done questions in the wrong order. You'll probably be able to use common sense here, and can reassure them that they should be all right so long as they make it clear to the examiner what they've done. If the query has needed a longer than usual response, it's worth mentioning what it was about to other invigilators in the room.

Remember that other students will notice if an invigilator is spending time with one student, and may wrongly assume the student is getting unfair help. This is another reason why it is important to keep interaction with students to a minimum. When one student can't understand a question on the paper, it's likely that others will have a problem as well, and this makes it doubly important for invigilators to be consistent in saying, "I can't help" and moving on. Otherwise, you may see candidates looking round to ask for help from someone they see as a "friendly invigilator" – even if the invigilator is not actually helping. Or, seeing some students appear to be getting help, a forest of hands may go up. When you see a fellow invigilator speaking to a student, keep an eye on what's happening behind them, and what that student does when the invigilator walks away. It's a point where students may try and communicate, thinking they're not being watched.

Communication

In direct contrast to exam students who are not allowed to communicate, invigilators have to be aware of each other and exchange information. Doing this without disturbing candidates is a tall order. When invigilators are moving between different areas of a large hall, it helps to share information about which students have been spoken to about behaviour. An exercise book on the invigilators' table is useful for recording minor behaviour issues which do not merit a formal malpractice report. This avoids a student getting lots of low-level warnings from different people without it ever getting properly dealt with, and provides a written record for other exam team members. Allocating invigilators to their own particular section of the hall can also help.

Later, we'll cover instructing students using signs rather than sound. It's useful for invigilators to develop simple sign language to share what they're doing or what is needed. A **T** gesture might mean "this student needs a toilet break". Or hands cycling round each other could indicate that you're going to move and need another invigilator to take your place.

You probably will need to speak to fellow invigilators sometimes. Needless to say you'll be trying to whisper, but some whispers are very loud. Don't be afraid to tell each other if this is the case; you can always practice outside the exam hall. Keep facing the students so you can still see them, but it's a good idea to shield your mouth – especially if you're referring to particular students or indeed other invigilators.

The more you work together, the easier it becomes to understand each other. You may find students using the same signs back to you when they want a pen or a calculator, for example. But don't make the sign language too involved, as it can then become a distraction.

Staying alert

If you're in a school or college with few behaviour management problems and a lot of small, uncomplicated exams, staying attentive can be a real issue. It's easy to lose focus. After lunch on a warm afternoon, you may even come near to falling asleep. On the grounds that you won't be able to manage behaviour properly if you're in a daze, here are a few tips to help you stay alert:

~ Move around the exam hall at regular intervals. The ICE booklet instructs invigilators to move frequently, but in some small venues it can be less disruptive to stay in one spot. However, as well as helping with the overall task of invigilating, moving around at least some of the time will help you to stay awake. In terms of managing behaviour, it helps that students are aware that there are invigilators around them. Also, some shyer students feel self-conscious putting a hand up but will speak to an invigilator who is close by. If possible, have one or more invigilators at the back of the room, too.

~ While some centres require invigilators to stand throughout the exam, others may allow you to sit for a small, quiet exam, provided you can easily see all the candidates. In some cases, sitting on a desk gives extra height and better visibility. (A tennis umpire's chair would be even better!) Be wary of sitting down if you're feeling sleepy, in case you nod off. And make sure you only sit on something sturdy. We know of invigilators who have had tables collapse under them during an exam.

~ Make sure you get a break. This is often easier said than done, we know. At the height of the exam season, what with extra times and clashes, you may go straight from the morning to the afternoon session without any time off. You may feel you simply have to put up with this, but you need at least a short break if you're to function properly. Don't feel awkward about asking your exam officer to relieve you for five minutes, for example.

~ Try to keep your focus on exam issues while you invigilate. As you move round the exam hall, you can look for specific issues on each circuit, such as any signs of phones in pockets, whether students have black pens, or if anyone has written on a hand. There may not be any issues in a quiet exam with only one or two students, so in that case having an alternative mental activity can help you to stay alert. But do make sure your eyes are always on the candidates. Having said that, some of us find it much easier than others to live with our thoughts. If being silent for hours drives you mad, invigilating probably isn't the right job for you!

~ Resist temptation. Be a role model for candidates for good conduct in exams. Invigilators who feel themselves getting bored can be tempted to read exam papers, check their time sheets, check their phones for messages or send a surreptitious text, whisper to fellow invigilators, or potter with things in the exam room. Without realising it, you may fidget, hum, jangle the keys in your pocket. Or even, as with the invigilator who fiddled with the cigarette lighter in his pocket, set fire to your trousers. Remember, you have to give your whole attention to the task. Moreover, if you distract students with noise or movement (or flames!) you're not just spoiling their concentration, you make it less likely that they'll listen when you tell them off for causing distractions.

~ Drinking water can aid concentration, so have a water bottle with you. Centres have different policies on whether invigilators are allowed hot drinks in the exam room. From the invigilator's perspective, this can help alertness in longer exams where no breaks are possible. But drinks must be managed discreetly, for example in a lidded travel mug, and not allowed anywhere near papers. Make sure there's somewhere safe to put your mug or bottle down when you respond to a hand going up.

Proactive invigilating

Proactive invigilators actively look for things they can do to improve the running of an exam, and constantly observe students to check for malpractice. If that sounds Big Brother-ish, it doesn't have to be. If you're moving frequently and quietly around the exam hall, as you're required to do, you can observe candidates discreetly, without making them feel you don't trust any of them an inch. Students who are working at their papers won't notice; but those who keep looking up and around will be aware of your attention. You'll soon know the difference between the appearance of a student who is working on their paper, and the angle of the head when they're not.

I observed a girl at the back of the exam hall very focused on something she was doing with her hands under her desk. I was convinced she had a phone and was texting, and moved rapidly to challenge her. As I bent to speak, I realised she was in fact absorbed in scratching off her nail polish! I smiled, and withdrew.

34

Sometimes a student is clearly distressed. It is difficult for invigilators to witness, but being proactive doesn't mean diving in at every opportunity. Be careful not to "fuss". If there is an ongoing situation such as a bereavement in their lives, hopefully you'll already have been told, and given advice on how to deal with it. If you don't know anything, and they aren't distracting others, it's probably best to give them a few minutes to calm themselves down if they can. Some people show every passing emotion, while others only show an emotion when they're feeling it really deeply. Unless you know the student well, it's hard to judge whether it's right to intervene.

Try asking: "Are you OK to carry on?" or, "What can I do to help?" If you're really concerned and there are enough invigilators you may be able to offer a short, supervised time outside the examination room. But this will depend on centre policy, as will your reaction if a student gives up on their exam and goes to sleep. We have met heated debate in our training sessions about whether waking a sleeping candidate is giving unfair help. You will need to check if there's a chance they are seriously unwell. Watching their behaviour before they put their head down should provide clues. But if you wake them in order to urge them to work, this might be considered to be malpractice. You will, however, definitely have to wake a candidate up if they are snoring!

You only need to intervene with a student who's doodling or doing something creative with their eraser or name label, if it's distracting others or they are actively trying to draw attention to what they're doing. You may need to make a judgement call on that, though. If the student who is doing something borderline is someone you know can be difficult, you might decide it will be less disruptive to keep a close eye on the situation. You may only need to intervene if the behaviour continues for more than a minute or two, or if it escalates so that it is clearly causing a problem.

Occasionally you may have a very anxious student in the exam hall, who repeatedly asks questions: "Is this where I sign my name? Can I use a rubber? Can I write on both sides of the answer paper?" The answers may be obvious, but you will need to reply briefly and calmly in a way which helps them settle down. If you know a student gets anxious, try and make sure you get to them quickly if their hand goes up. If you can, a smile and a check that they have everything they need before the exam starts can be helpful. Be aware of them if you have to speak to the group as a whole about behaviour. They may feel any criticism personally, even where they weren't involved, and need reassurance.

You might occasionally need a different approach when invigilating candidates with access arrangements for emotional or behavioural issues. The line between giving appropriate support and giving an unfair advantage isn't always clear-cut, but your exam officer can guide you on dealing with individual students.

Cheating

Exam boards tend to speak of "malpractice" rather than cheating, Malpractice includes cheating, but also covers all breaking of the rules and maladministration. In this section, we focus on deliberate cheating, that is, any attempt by candidates to gain an unfair advantage by copying another's work, bringing in notes, or getting access to additional information during the exam.

An internet search for "exam cheats" produces an alarming range of possibilities, but in our experience, actual cheating among school or college students is rare. While this could be put down to candidates simply being too good at it, if invigilators are picking up numerous other instances of malpractice, they should also have picked up cheating if it was going on. Most students are honest, and since they know the invigilators are watching, don't take the risk of cheating even if they're tempted. However, there will be exceptions, and some things to keep an eye out for are students who:

~ look around – are they reading another candidate's paper?

~ do something under the desk – have they a phone or notes?

~ fiddle with their sleeves – is there writing on their arm?

~ put a hand in their pocket – are they trying to access notes or a phone?

~ keep a hand over one ear for a long period – have they got a wire in there?

~ focus intently on something other than their exam paper

~ check where the invigilator is, but don't put a hand up

~ have an unusual body position – is that hand clasped behind their neck showing a message to the student behind?

These signs don't automatically mean the student is cheating, but they do indicate areas of the exam hall you'll keep an unobtrusive eye on. That way, you'll see if the student who glances round starts trying to read someone else's paper, and can intervene. If you think a student may be trying to read another person's paper, go and stand near them. For proof of cheating, you will need to observe whether they are on the same page as the person they've watched, and particularly whether they make any alterations.

In our invigilation training for Exam Team Development, we often ask the question: if you were a student who wanted to cheat in your exam centre, how would you do it? This helps exam teams to identify areas where they need to tighten up to keep exams secure. For example, could students be consulting notes when taken for a toilet break? It is good practice to search toilet cubicles before and after students have used them, since it has been known for notes to be concealed there. Since notes or phones can easily be concealed on the person and retrieved during a toilet visit, only a complete ban on toilet breaks will prevent this completely. As mentioned above, this can in itself be problematic.

Your exam officer will guide you in what to do if you suspect malpractice, but think about how and when you will speak to the student if this happens. You may be able to nip a situation in the bud if you are observant and quick: "I'm sure you wouldn't deliberately look at someone else's work", could be followed by a description of the behaviour: "but you appeared to be looking across at another desk", and then instruction about what they need to do: "so please keep focused on your own work so there can be no misunderstanding in future." Then move away, but keep an eye on the candidate, and quietly ask other invigilators to watch them as well, if you can. It is always easier to prove suspected malpractice if more than one invigilator has observed the same thing.

Managing teachers

As we've mentioned, there are strict rules about which members of staff may enter the examination room and what they are permitted to do there. You will need to keep up to date with current rules, and know which staff your Head of Centre has authorised to be present - for example, to help with discipline. It helps if teachers and other centre staff have been reminded about the regulations on who may enter the exam room, and if a notice can be prominently displayed. Some centres put a copy of the relevant JCQ notice up in the staff room and/or outside the main exam room.

But there are occasionally staff members who are unfamiliar with current rules, or even who try to bend the rules, for example, by giving encouragement to a student. So invigilators may find they have to challenge a teacher who has come into the exam room. This isn't easy, particularly for an inexperienced invigilator with a long-standing, perhaps senior, member of staff. Approaching with a smile, and "I'm sorry, I'm not allowed to let you …" is usually enough. If the teacher objects, or disagrees with your interpretation of the rules, tactfully point them to the JCQ notice or similar, or refer them to your exam officer. The invigilator has responsibility within the exam hall, and must make sure that there is no malpractice.

More difficult is the case where the member of staff can legitimately interact with a student, for example in a practical exam, or if they have been requested to discipline a disruptive student. Again, the line between what's allowed and what is inappropriate help or encouragement isn't always easy to draw.

For some access arrangements – for example, if a candidate has a practical assistant or sign language interpreter – you may be invigilating alongside support staff. Strict rules apply to access arrangements, and you will receive additional training for invigilating under these circumstances. As before, the invigilator has to intervene if a staff member breaks the rules, but it isn't easy to do.

We recommend talking through issues like this with the exam team, and practising what to say and how to say it without creating bad feeling. Also, your exam officer can speak to senior management if there is an issue with a particular staff member.

CHAPTER FIVE

Managing Behaviour with Individuals

Managing behaviour is a complex business. The best approach is to take action to avoid problems arising in the first place, but that is not always possible. The tricky balancing act you have to perform here is one you share with other staff. On the one hand, you will be taking an authoritative, firm approach to behaviour. On the other, you will empathise with students who are under stress or simply not coping well with the business of growing up, for whatever reason.

Stay calm

Some teenagers are very skilled at winding adults up. But if you can, it's important to model calm, positive, adult behaviour both inside and outside the exam hall, whatever is thrown at you. In the classroom, teachers will try to manage difficult situations in a restorative way, that is, to help students be aware of who is affected by their behaviour and how they can put things right. It's difficult to do this in a short, quiet conversation in the exam room, but you may be able to use this approach with a student after the exam: "Who is affected by what you did? How can you put it right?"

As we've said, it's key for invigilators to develop a confident, calm, reassuring presence in the exam hall. Some of this can only come with experience, knowing the rules and ways of dealing with problems. However, presence can also come simply from adopting a more confident body language and tone of voice. Those who have an assertive, though not aggressive manner, are less likely to be challenged. It's worth practising this in front of a mirror - or perhaps the family pet! Or you could ask someone you trust to assess you starting an imaginary examination.

Low-level disruption

The most common misbehaviour in the exam hall is low-level disruption. Although the school or college may have briefed students about behaviour in exams, they may not appreciate that "communication" covers exchanging smiles or gestures, as well as actually whispering or speaking to somebody else. Candidates may be restless and/or noisy, perhaps tapping feet or playing with a desk label. Students who have serious difficulties with concentration may well be taking their exams in a supported environment. But you may still have students who find it very hard to sit still or to concentrate for long periods. They may get unsettled very easily by outside noise or someone near them getting attention. You may also have disruptive students whose bravado is hiding the fear that they'll lose face if they try and then fail. Ideally, your exam officer will change where potential trouble-makers are seated to minimise the risk of challenging behaviour.

However much you try to understand the stresses on students and empathise with the teenage mind, your job is to keep the rules and enable all the students in front of you to do their best in this exam. You therefore have to stop low-level disruption before it escalates.

When to intervene

It's a fine art to decide if and when to intervene. Students are told to "Face the front", so you need to deal with someone who keeps turning round. But what if their head is at a 45 degree angle to the front? Does it matter if they turn round if they're at the back anyway? Some students are simply trying to get your attention, and will give up and get on with their work if you ignore them. Others will begin small and keep going until you do something – so it's best to intervene early.

Some behaviours aren't terribly serious in themselves, but will spread if they're ignored. The student who keeps looking round eventually makes eye contact with a friend, then mouths words at them, and others join in. Perhaps the best advice is that you stay aware of which students are potentially misbehaving. Let them know you're aware, even if you decide not to take any action at that point. With experience, you will be able to decide when to step in.

Keep your fellow invigilators informed, and be aware of the incidents your fellow invigilators are dealing with. A brief, whispered exchange of information about an incident, or a quick scan of what an invigilator has recorded about the incident, is enough to keep everyone in the team up to date. That way, the team can continue to invigilate the whole group consistently and effectively.

Keep it quiet

Your aim is to intervene with the least possible interaction. Think of it as a "ladder of intervention", where you try and stay at the lowest level possible, but have steps you can take if necessary. If you see students cheating, or there's other serious malpractice, obviously you need to speak to them straight away. Otherwise, your first intervention can be gestures and tactics such as:

~ finger on lips for quiet

~ nodding or shaking head

~ eye contact – widen eyes or raise eyebrows if necessary to look surprised

~ thumbs up

~ mouthing instructions

~ an open hand with fingers downwards to indicate not swinging on a chair ("four on the floor")

~ an open flat hand at 45 degrees to indicate the need to stop or calm down

~ standing between a student and someone they're staring at

The first few points on this list are obvious ones you'll use naturally. The others are more specific for an exam situation, and are often surprisingly effective. However, be warned, if they're done aggressively, young people may well ignore you. Accompanying them with a smile, or just half a smile, makes them more likely to work. The non-verbal message you're trying to get across is: "You know the rules, you know what you're doing, you know what you need to do. I expect compliance."

It can help to give students "take-up time". When new invigilators first encounter poor behaviour, their instinct may be forcibly to tell the student off and expect instant obedience. True, that approach can work with some students, though you may end up unnecessarily upsetting a student who is being distracted rather than malicious. The real trouble-makers will see it as a challenge if you stand over them hissing, "Do it! Now!" Allowing "take-up time" is much more effective. Make eye contact, use an appropriate gesture, and then turn your attention away. This allows them time to think about it and to feel they're choosing to stop the behaviour, rather than being bossed about and losing face. When they have complied, it's often good to give a smile or thumbs-up.

It's particularly difficult to move away if you are on the receiving end of an insolent stare or muttered obscenity. Even if you personally are not bothered by bad language, the school or college may have a "zero tolerance" policy on it. Not responding can feel like you're losing face and letting them "get away with it". But remember that mantra: how can I help all these students to have the best exam experience possible? Having a confrontation during an exam is rarely a good way forward.

If a comment was made under the breath and no-one else was disturbed, "tactical ignoring" may be the most helpful option. You can always record the incident and take action at the end of the exam if necessary. If it cannot be ignored, a shake of the head or a brief comment such as, "You know that language is not acceptable here," may be enough. Or a warning might be necessary. If possible, keep the exchange between you and the student, rather than making it public to the whole group.

When you walk away from a student who's causing concern, swizzle round to catch what they're doing behind your back. Once you have moved away, you should still "invigilate from a distance". Let your gaze sweep across students who are concerning you, but only let it rest on them if they're doing something they shouldn't. You're then giving the message, "I'm still aware of you, but I won't bother you if you behave properly."

Time for a word

If the above doesn't work, or you've frequently had to convey the same message to the same student, or the behaviour is seriously disruptive, you will need to say something. Certain phrases and approaches help, but make them your own, and try not to sound angry (even if you are!)

~ Go right up to the student and come down to their level if possible

~ Address them by name

45

~ Be assertive, not aggressive

~ Describe the problem behaviour

~ Remind them they are under exam conditions. You can use such phrases as: "This is not acceptable", "You know how to behave". "Respect other students who are trying to work".

~ Give your instruction, saying "please"

~ Say "thank-you"

~ Walk away to give "take-up time"

If appropriate, you can be empathetic: "I can see you've finished, but others are still working". Or bring in something positive, such as, "You've worked really hard up to now, keep it going for five more minutes." "You concentrated very well in yesterday's exam, I know you can do it." If you've already got to know students, it'll be easier to find your own form of words without making the situation worse. Of course you need to keep any additional phrases like this to a minimum, and they must be directed towards behaviour not offering any advice or comment on the candidate's work.

If you've had to speak to a student, it's important to record the fact. You are required to record any irregularities in the exam hall, and there may be a notebook in the hall for all invigilators to use, or you may have your own notebook, or both. These are ways of recording who has been spoken to and why, although it may go no further if they then behave. It's a marker that they've had a verbal warning, and they'll soon learn that the next stage is that they'll be reported.

Your exam officer will explain the procedures for reporting misbehaviour, consistent with the centre's behaviour policy. There'll be a difference according to whether this is an internal exam or whether malpractice has to be reported to the awarding body. Try to avoid telling candidates "You will be disqualified", as this decision does not rest with you. However, you can say that you will report them to the exam officer, or where there is malpractice, that they will be reported to the awarding body and risk being disqualified. If you tell a candidate you will report them, remember to follow it through.

If students do improve behaviour after you've spoken to them, it can be worth mentioning it to them quietly at the end of that exam or at the beginning of their next one. This could just be a thumbs up or a mouthed "Thank you" – you don't want to embarrass them.

If a student has made a big effort to improve behaviour, tell their teacher, Head of Year or pastoral manager, so they can pass it on at the right time. You can note improvements in behaviour in the exam room logbook, as well as recording problems which arise.

Now it's serious

When you see or hear serious misbehaviour going on, take a second to check and reflect before approaching the student. It will help if a fellow invigilator stands nearby, both to observe your intervention and to remind other candidates in the vicinity to keep attending to their work. However, make sure there is still an invigilator watching the group as a whole.

When you speak to the student, as before, address them by name, speaking quietly and calmly near their ear, and not getting into a power struggle. Forms of words which help are: "I need you to ..."; "What do you need to do to put this right?"; "Put this right, please".

You can give a choice as long as you are setting the limits: "If you choose to x, then you will have chosen y" is better than, "If you do x then y will happen". For example you might say: "If you choose to communicate with other candidates then you will have chosen to be removed from the examination room". If they continue and they have to be removed, you will be able to do it "more in sorrow than anger," which may well help to reduce any further disruption as the student leaves. Remember to check on what supervision arrangements apply in that exam, so that students can continue to be fully supervised for the appropriate period after they're withdrawn from the room. Usually, you will have summoned the exam officer if a student needs to be removed, and he or she will take over.

There are some situations where you will need to act decisively. Obviously, if there is serious misconduct, such as cheating, then a choice is not appropriate. You will have received guidance from your exam officer about the procedures to follow if you spot cheating. Rarely, a student will be seriously disruptive and need immediate removal before any help you have summoned can arrive. As long as you have a fellow invigilator to take over, try saying, "I need you to come with me now to sort this out, please," then walk out slowly **without looking back**. In the unlikely event they don't actually follow, you can go straight to get help.

You should know how to call for help from the exam officer or a senior member of staff – make sure you know exactly what to do before you're left to invigilate on your own. New invigilators also need to know this, in case a more experienced fellow invigilator has to leave the room temporarily. However brief your training, do find this out.

Decisions about misbehaviour, whether minor or serious, are finely balanced. Whatever happens, make your choice and try not to worry about it. If you have genuinely done your best to handle a situation in which there was no one right answer, a good exam officer will back you up. Later, when things have settled down, it's worth reflecting with the exam officer and other invigilators what if anything you could do differently if the situation arises again.

Prevention

If you know the students, then getting them to behave, or even to leave the exam room, should be easier. The way you behave towards students before a crisis comes up is really important. Get this right and your job will be so much simpler. Treat them well when you're invigilating and use every opportunity to build relationships with them between exams. You can often have a friendly chat in between exams if you're supervising students who have a clash, for example. You shouldn't be having conversations with a student you're taking for a toilet break during an exam – unless it's about a behavioural issue. But accompanying them with a friendly smile or word will stand you in good stead if you need to deal with them at other times.

As we say in **Things the invigilator can do** in Chapter 2, if you get involved in the life of the school or college, you'll get to know students and the right approach to take with them. We know this isn't possible for invigilators who work across many different centres, but it's true that students will view you differently if they've seen you around a lot.

A charming but lively GCSE student put his hand up.

"How long is this exam, Miss?" he whispered.

It was on the board and his paper, but I told him.

"Is part two this afternoon?"

"Yes."

"Are you doing that one?"

"Yes I am."

"Do you like invigilating, Miss?"

I had to smile at how expertly he'd led me up to having a conversation with him.

"Ask me after the exam," I whispered, and moved quickly away.

CHAPTER SIX

Managing Behaviour in Groups

The sight of a hall full of hundreds of teenagers can be daunting if you're not used to it. Even if they are all well-behaved, it takes skill to get their attention as a group and to manage their comings and goings. Ideally, your exam officer will appoint one or more senior invigilators who are happy to be responsible for this upfront role, and less experienced invigilators are unlikely to be in charge of a large group. However, you might find yourself unexpectedly at the front having to finish a large exam, if the senior invigilator is detained elsewhere, or the exam officer is dealing with an emergency, for example. And even if you're not up front, you'll play a part in managing the group's behaviour, and there are many things you can do to help. So this section is for you too.

The advice given above for managing individuals can be adapted and used for groups, especially the need to be authoritative, calm and clear, and to work together as a team. You may think you need to tackle the whole group at one go, but in fact sorting out individuals often does the job better. However, there are times when you need to manage behaviour in the group as a whole.

Addressing the group

You may be an experienced invigilator, but managing large groups of teenagers takes additional skills. Having a few techniques up your sleeve will help you to approach the task more confidently.

If you're not used to speaking in public, practise effective voice projection. You're aiming for clarity rather than sheer volume, and try to avoid screaming or screeching. If the exam room is already quiet, a low voice will carry well. If a lot of people are talking, you will need to raise the volume, but try not to shout; it will sound as if you're losing control. As soon as the noise level comes down, so should your voice. Standing up straight, slowing down your words, and deepening your voice, can all help to convey authority. Setting the right tone will avoid winding students up. Raising your eyebrows for a second is more effective than looking anxious, and humour can help to defuse potentially difficult situations.

The two main times you will be addressing the students as a group are at the start and end of the exam. We'll assume for the moment that there aren't other exams with different starting and finishing times in the same room. If there are, you need to keep instructions to a minimum and follow up any issues outside the exam hall.

If behaviour is good, simply give the necessary instructions clearly and slowly, adjusting to the acoustics of the room. Other invigilators can help by cupping a hand to their ear if their section of the room can't hear. For very large numbers, consider using a microphone, and/or a smart board display. It's frustrating and can harm their chances if students miss important instructions. You'll have been briefed on how to make announcements accessible for any candidates in the main hall with hearing or sight disabilities. But also be aware of students for whom English is not a first language, and keep instructions straightforward.

Students should know that they are under exam conditions from the moment they enter the exam room until they have left it, so that it is a place of complete silence. However, you may find some of them try to talk the minute the exam ends. If so, you will need to get their attention.

As we said in Chapter 3, address them by name with a confident "Year Eleven!" (or as appropriate). Then pause for take-up time before repeating the command if necessary. "Year Eleven, may I have your attention". Once noise levels reduce, drop the volume slightly, as mentioned above.

If they don't quieten down, be careful to stay calm so as not to escalate the situation. If the exam hasn't begun, you could warn them that it can't start without silence, so it will finish late. At the end, you could say, "You are still under exam conditions. I need you to be silent now, please, so you'll be able to leave on time", or a variation on this. Standing waiting, with occasional reminders that they'll be dismissed once they're quiet, is usually effective. After all, they want to escape! You should always dismiss them one row at a time, and can miss out rows where there is disruption. If only one or two are misbehaving, keep them back to deal with after the others have gone. Make a note of their names before the group goes, though, as very difficult students may simply walk out.

"No one's going until you're silent" can also work, because you can carry it through. One thing not to do under any circumstances, is to make empty threats. If you say "No one is leaving until I find out who is whistling", you are all going to be there for a very long time.

Working as a team

Although the exam officer or senior invigilator at the front is in authority and sets the tone by their voice and body language, the whole team has a role in managing the behaviour of the group. Invigilators elsewhere in the room can direct students to listen to instructions from the front, and repeat them if necessary. If they see that the person at the front is concerned about a particular student or area of the hall, they can approach from a different direction or move to stand nearby. This doesn't have to be done intrusively, but lets the students know the invigilators are monitoring them.

As we've stressed, it's crucial for invigilators to work as a team and communicate with each other. The more you have a common strategy, the more effective you will be and the more you will enjoy the job. Good teamwork requires good planning to make sure nothing is missed. Don't underestimate the importance of debriefing at the end of every exam; if you can all work out what makes things better or worse, each exam is likely to be better than the last.

Coughers, whistlers and knuckle-crackers

It's particularly important to have agreed a plan for tackling issues in the whole group. Epidemics of deliberate coughing, etc. can easily spread if not nipped in the bud, and they're very distracting for the other candidates. Since some students have a genuine cough, it's hard to know when it's being done deliberately to cause trouble. However, it's usually easy to identify the cougher. If they persist, you can ask if they would like some water, or warn them they're distracting others. Someone cracking knuckles is usually easy to spot as well, since they physically have to pull their fingers. Whistling is more of a problem. As you may have discovered, it's very hard to tell exactly where the sound is coming from. However, with vigilance and teamwork, you should be able to track down the culprit(s). Here are some tips which may be worth trying.

If you're at the front, try to avoid looking interested and observe only out of the corner of your eye. The whistlers want to engage you in a game, and you're playing into their hands if you immediately spring to attention. Also, if they don't think you've noticed, they may make it more obvious, which makes them easier to spot. Try angling your head towards a different part of the hall to the one you think the sound came from, while glancing back at the area of concern.

We call this an "eye dummy", and it works best when done at a distance. You may then spot the culprit, or at least be able to narrow down where the sound is coming from. You can then – still casually and as if you haven't noticed – adjust your position and see if you can narrow things down still further. Fellow invigilators should observe from other positions in the hall, and also move to narrow things down.

Once one person thinks it's funny to whistle, cough, or crack a knuckle, their friends will soon join in. If you try and spot first one and then the other, you'll be running round in circles. Try to catch one of the individuals, approach them, speak to them and record their name. Hopefully it will be a warning to the others. If not, systematically try to track down the next person and do the same.

If a significant number of students are joining in, you may need to make a short, calm announcement. Remind them that they are under exam conditions and that this behaviour is unacceptable and must stop now. In our experience, one of the culprits will inevitably respond by making the noise again at that point, but not very subtly, so you have a good chance of catching them!

Record the incident and report to the exam officer, who may wish to ask the appropriate member of staff to speak to the group before their next exam.

What to do if you lose control

If your invigilation team have trained in behaviour management and are fully supported by the school or college, loss of control shouldn't happen. Your centre will have strategies in place to resolve escalating situations very quickly, and your exam officer should have briefed you on what to do if they cannot immediately respond to your request for help - perhaps because of a crisis elsewhere. So it is very rare for an invigilator to be left to cope with a badly behaving group. But just in case you ever find yourself in a situation where the strategies we have suggested aren't working, and you feel as if the whole group is out of control, is there anything you can do?

If your normal way of summoning help is not being answered, send a fellow invigilator, even if it temporarily leaves you one short or on your own with the situation. Record the names of students who are being disruptive. You may not be able to deal with them during the exam, but you can make sure there are consequences afterwards. Note if there are students who are behaving well, so they are not included in the consequences.

If intervening with individuals isn't working, you can make a general announcement: "You are still under exam conditions and there must be no communicating …" "This behaviour is not acceptable …" "I need you to …" Try not to look as if you are upset. A little acting may be needed in order to appear confident, but it will help. Remember that this situation is MOST unlikely to happen, especially in a public examination.

In the unlikely event you are unable to ensure exam conditions and no help has arrived, you could consider abandoning the exam. Warn the students that unless behaviour improves, you will end the exam. They will all be reported to the awarding body and are likely to score zero in this, and other exams they've sat for that awarding body. They may have to pay the exam's entrance fee, and will face serious consequences with the school or college. You may still need to keep them under supervision.

Afterwards, debrief the situation fully with the exam officer, and examine how it can be prevented in future. You'll have to write a report, but also make sure you can "offload" your feelings about it. It's a horrible experience, but it isn't your fault, so don't let it stop you developing your skills and confidence as an invigilator.

CHAPTER SEVEN

Managing the End of the Exam

As the end of an exam gets closer, the invigilators get ready for another burst of action. There are many practical tasks to do — collecting papers, recovering equipment, dismissing students. There may be several different exams going on, all with different official finish times, as well as students granted extra time, or who've arrived late. So the practical tasks have to be done with a minimum of disruption, while continuing to supervise behaviour both of the students whose exam is over and those who are still working.

In addition, there will be students who decide that they've finished their exam, even though they haven't used the whole time. For some — including Winston Churchill — this point may come within a few minutes of the start!

I wrote my name at the top of the page. I wrote down the number of the question I. After much reflection I put a bracket round it thus (I). But thereafter I could not think of anything connected with it that was either relevant or true. Incidentally there arrived from nowhere in particular a blot and several smudges. I gazed for two whole hours at this sad spectacle: and then merciful ushers collected my piece of foolscap with all the others and carried it up to the Headmaster's table.   Winston Churchill *My Early Life*

So in the same way that it helps to have extra invigilators available and specific roles allocated at the start of the exam, it's useful to plan how invigilators are used at the end. This will be one of the responsibilities of a senior invigilator, if your centre has one. Perhaps suggesting invigilation teams should learn a lesson from Formula 1 pit stops is going too far, but it does help when everyone can do their allotted task quickly and smoothly. If invigilators stick to a pattern for collecting papers, it makes the job of sorting much easier, and also gets the students out of the hall much quicker. Regularly rotating the different tasks among invigilators helps to ensure everyone becomes experienced and capable.

Things which help maintain good behaviour at the end of the exam might include:

~ Refusing toilet breaks during the last 15-30 minutes

~ Making sure at least one experienced invigilator stands at the front of the room to focus on student behaviour while the others are collecting papers. Some students could still be working when others leave.

~ If possible, especially in large exams, having another invigilator at the back of the room specifically focusing on behaviour.

~ Not letting up. Being more lenient may not seem to matter if everyone has finished, or during the pause while you check you have collected all the scripts before dismissing students. But one lesson from general classroom management is that the way a class leaves a lesson is the way they will begin the next time. So maintaining exam conditions right up until students leave the exam hall reinforces the message: "this is how we behave in exams".

~ If possible, have an extra pair of hands at the end. If an invigilator has to leave the exam room to enable students to collect their bags at the end of the exam, it leaves the invigilation team one short at a key point.

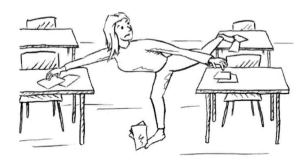

~ If bags have had to be left in the exam room, ensure an invigilator supervises students as they collect their things. They'll find it hard not to chat about the exam, even if they can see others are still working.

If an exam is running late for whatever reason, students may be restless because they're worried about missing buses etc. It may be worth having a "Plan B" in place. For example in internal exams, students can be asked to leave their papers on the desk or to hand their paper in as they leave the hall. However, this needs supervising carefully to make sure no one leaves without handing a paper in. This must not be done for public exams.

Time warnings

There is no requirement in the ICE booklet to give a time warning to candidates as the end of the exam approaches, although the regulations for some types of examination do still require warnings to be given. The University of Cambridge IGCSE is one example. Exam officers may have their own centre policy on this, which you will need to follow. You can report back to them if you find giving or not giving warnings is unhelpful in a given situation. For example, a 5 minute warning can break the atmosphere in the exam room, with students looking around as if the exam has actually ended. Or if there are several exams, it can be distracting when invigilators are giving 5 minute warnings as well as announcing the end of each exam. Things can also get complicated if there are a number of candidates in the exam room who get extra time.

As well as being clear what the regulations say for the particular exam, invigilators must make sure they are consistent, so that students know whether they'll get the time warning, and if they're told they will, that someone remembers to do it.

Pens down

One person will have responsibility for stopping each exam at the right time, but it's important for other invigilators to keep an eye on the clock too. You need to be aware, not just of the main finish times but those with extra time, clashes, and late starters. It certainly helps to have these listed on the board at the front, and some invigilators find it helpful to make their own list, as illustrated. This can include other points which might get forgotten.

    10.00 Geography finish. 2 have extra time
    10.04 Jake finishes – send to reception
    10.15 Helga finishes, remind re dictionary
    10.30 History finishes – keep Jade – CLASH
    10.45 French finishes – don't seal papers

"Unless you have been given extra time, stop now," is often the safest instruction, in case someone who should have extra time has been missed on the register. Keep instructions and comments to a minimum if there are still students working. Asking students to leave "in silence" is more effective than a request to leave "quietly".

It's important to give praise if students have behaved well. A thank you for helping the exam go smoothly, or for coming in really quietly, or whatever has been done well, can easily be given before dismissal. If there are other exams still going on, this can be limited to "Thank you, well done." Or start the next exam with a brief positive comment on what went well last time, which will set a good tone.

If exams are finished by your exam officer, but they haven't been present during the exam, briefly pass on comments about behaviour. It's an encouragement for everyone if you pass on positive comments. If you're reporting problems, it helps the students see that you're taking it seriously. It's also good for students to hear the exam officer backing the invigilation team by saying poor behaviour is not acceptable.

CHAPTER EIGHT

Special Situations

Access arrangements, one-to-one, supported environment

Being assigned to invigilate students with access arrangements brings an additional set of regulations, which your exam officer will brief you on. As we noted earlier, you may be invigilating while someone else provides support, for example as a practical assistant. You will need to be familiar with exactly what they can, and cannot, do, and intervene if necessary. The invigilator can act as a scribe, prompter or reader where a candidate is accommodated separately, so you could be on your own both invigilating and providing support. The orange JCQ booklet has a memory aide about these roles, and your exam officer will provide a copy of this or its equivalent in the exam room so all staff and the student too can be clear about the rules.

If the student has a particular behaviour issue, you should be supported by a member of staff who is already familiar with managing their behaviour, at least until you yourself get to know the student. The invigilator's role here is to ensure that the exam is run under the correct exam conditions. It isn't always easy for teaching assistants to switch from their close, supportive role with a student, to only providing assistance within strict limits. The invigilator therefore needs not only to understand what the regulations about access arrangements say, but to be clear with teaching assistants what these mean in practice.

Some invigilators find that boredom is the biggest problem when there are single or very few students, since any paperwork is quickly done, and some of these students have extra time, too. It is worth advance planning so that you can take a short break in a long exam, and keep your concentration levels high.

Sometimes, where a centre identifies a number of potentially disruptive students, they will sit their exams in a small group together. This has the advantage of removing them from the main group, where they might cause problems. However, they can be even less likely to make a proper attempt at an exam when surrounded by that peer group. If invigilators can manage such students effectively in the main hall, so much the better.

Art and other practical exams

Practical timed tests in subjects such as Art or ICT are normally invigilated by a teacher, who is able to provide appropriate technical assistance and supervision. Additional invigilators may be deployed at the exam officer's discretion, so the group can be supervised if the teacher has to advise an individual candidate.

You may therefore be invigilating in an exam where the teacher is in charge, rather than a member of your exam team. While teachers will know the general rules, they are also providing technical assistance, and are unlikely to be as focused on exam regulations as you are. Although practical tests have to be carried out under formal exam conditions, and candidates are not allowed to communicate in any way with, ask for help from, or give help to another candidate, in practice, these tests do feel different to exams in the main hall. For example, the teacher can legitimately speak to candidates. Students are able to move around, and might have to speak to another candidate to request an item of equipment. They may leave the room unsupervised to access a particular piece of equipment. This can give potentially disruptive students more opportunities to misbehave, but having a teacher present should mean that poor behaviour gets dealt with promptly.

Your role as an invigilator is the same as always, to make sure that all the relevant exam regulations are strictly adhered to. Yet you may have to make some difficult judgements. Is an Art candidate who says, "Can I have that colour?" and is told "You don't want to use that one, do you?" being given advice? At what point does a teacher's permitted technical assistance become unfair advice and malpractice? It is also less easy for invigilators to challenge such behaviours, since the teacher is the expert in the room, and is in charge of the exam. It is useful if the teacher has been tactfully briefed by the exam officer so that they understand that the invigilator has a duty to report any malpractice from adults and students.

If there are clear breaches of exam rules, you will need to take action, but it's also worth making a note of any incidents where you are not quite sure, so you can get guidance. Debriefing with your exam officer and fellow invigilators, and if possible, teachers themselves, will help you to be clear about what is permitted and how to tackle any issues.

On-screen tests

As with practical tests, the fact that on-screen exams are held away from the usual exam rooms can make them more difficult to invigilate. Students who are used to chatting to each other as they sit at computers may find it harder to adjust to now being under exam conditions.

For reasons of space, candidates may be seated alongside each other. Though there is a minimum distance allowed between seats, and they will be sitting different tests, it could be possible for them to see each other's screens and possibly comment to each other if invigilators are not extremely vigilant. It is worth reminding candidates at the start that they could be spoiling their own chances if they allow themselves to be distracted by someone else's screen.

The room lay out may mean that you have to turn your back on the rest of the candidates when one has a problem. They may legitimately have scrap paper for making notes about the test, but could pass a note to a friend if you are distracted. While there should be an IT specialist on hand to deal with any technical issues, you may get asked for help logging on or checking a password. You should get training in dealing with these situations, but it also helps to have extra invigilators on hand at the start of an exam to ensure candidates are kept under exam conditions.

You may find the style of on-screen tests helps with behaviour issues. A candidate advances through the test at their own pace, and once they have finished, may be able to leave.

Modern languages, music and media

If you are invigilating subjects with an audio and/or video component, you will be responsible for the technology as well as for ensuring exam conditions. The audio component may be delivered individually to candidates, as with A level music, or candidates may listen or watch as a group, as with a modern language GCSE. These exams are often relatively short, and their design tends to hold students' attention. This helps reduce behaviour issues.

It's important to familiarise yourself with the technology in case anything goes wrong, and to know how to summon appropriate help fast. If you're on your own, you might find it hard to enforce exam conditions while simultaneously trying to get a CD or DVD working again. In the absence of prompt help, a candidate may offer to fix the problem, and this might be the least bad solution.

Oral tests for language exams are conducted between teacher and student without invigilators present, but you may be asked to supervise students awaiting their test. They will be using the time to revise and prepare, so you won't speak to them much. But it is an opportunity to put names to faces, and be friendly and reassuring. This will help your interactions with them when they are in written exams.

In music exams, you'll see occasional tapping of feet or tapping on desks as students get involved with the music. If candidates have individual players, they can sometimes get carried away, even singing along. If other candidates are affected, you'll need to intervene, but this can usually be done with a smile and fingers to lips. Where everyone is listening to the same CD, they may respond as a group to a piece of music they recognise, or to a particularly vibrant rhythm. There'll be smiles and moving to the beat, which might not normally be appropriate behaviour in an exam, but somewhat difficult to police. Indeed you as the invigilator may find it hard not to tap your feet as well.

Your chief concern is ensure that all candidates get an equal chance to do their best in the exam, and that kind of impromptu response to the music won't present a threat to exam conditions. However, you do have to keep it low-key, and might need to use calm-down gestures to make sure students don't get carried away.

When you're asked to invigilate an exam with an audio or video component, do tell your exam officer if you think you might find the content difficult. For example, not everyone is comfortable watching war movies or horror films, but the exam might involve scenes from these being played several times over. Or if you are strongly affected by music, listening to pieces being played several times over might stop you focusing on the job.

Supervising clash students

During the exam season, you may be asked to supervise a student who has sat a paper early or who must be kept apart from other candidates. This can be one of the more enjoyable aspects of invigilating, as some students like to chat about their plans, interests and dreams. Whether or not they want to speak, demonstrating that you're a helpful, friendly invigilator can make life smoother in the exam hall.

If you are supervising a student over a lunch break, and have an afternoon exam to invigilate, do make sure you have had a chance to switch off and have your own lunch, otherwise it may be hard to concentrate.

CHAPTER NINE

Outside the Exam Room

Debriefing

Regular debriefing is very important if invigilators are to develop in the job. It gives a chance to swap ideas and exchange information about what has been good and what improvements could be made. If things have gone wrong, it helps to have somewhere to let off steam. It's a chance to learn both from what's gone well and what hasn't. If the invigilation team is focused on solving problems, then the whole process can be very constructive.

Even when there have been problems, saying, "This is what happened and this is what I did," can open up a discussion on what else could have been tried. Remember there aren't always simple right answers, and that hindsight is a wonderful thing. Invigilators are often working under urgent time pressures, and sometimes have to take instant decisions which turn out to be a mistake. If you can share the situation with fellow invigilators and/or the exam officer, and come up with a solution for the next time, you won't need to feel bad.

There may not be much time for debriefing at the height of the exam season. If invigilators are coming and going on different days and for different exams, they may see little of each other outside the exam hall. "Free time" between exams may be taken up with sorting papers or setting up the exam hall. The exam officer will be very busy, too, and however well-intentioned, may not have time to keep an eye on invigilators. It's therefore worth having a senior or experienced invigilator given responsibility for checking out how invigilators are doing and feeling. At the end of the exam season, there should be time to have a longer debriefing session, and this can throw up issues to be tackled in future training sessions.

If the school or college has behaviour management issues, and it's not an area of expertise for the exam officer, it is helpful for invigilators to have input on this issue from a member of senior staff or external trainers.

Safeguarding

As someone who works with young people in a school or college, you will have passed a Disclosure and Barring Service (DBS, previously Criminal Record Bureau) check. You will have received training so you understand your responsibilities in relation to child protection, and how to report any concerns you might have. While it's beyond the scope of this book to go into detail on this, some points are relevant to managing behaviour in exams.

Children and young people who are subjected to neglect, sexual, physical or emotional/psychological abuse, may show this in their behaviour. So be alert to any student in an exam who:

~ is unusually disruptive and angry

~ shows signs of violence

~ is tearful and has trouble concentrating

~ is inadequately dressed

~ never has any equipment

~ is late to or misses lots of exams

There may be many different and innocent reasons for these things, but an awareness of the importance of safeguarding means you can raise the question with your exam officer. Often, he or she will have been briefed by a teacher that a particular student has a problem.

Don't assume that somebody else in your school or college is bound to have noticed an issue about a particular student. It is your duty to make sure that your concern is passed on. At exam times, students may only attend when sitting their papers, so you may be the only adult who is aware of a problem. Also, you closely observe students as part of your role. You may pick up unusual behaviours, or notice those bruises, where a teacher in a busy classroom might not. Make sure you record any unusual or concerning matters in the exam record book, so that any patterns can be picked up.

Your exam officer may be able to brief you about vulnerable students, so you can be aware in your dealings with them. However, sometimes such information is confidential, and won't be passed to you. We know you'll strive to be calm, respectful and positive towards the young people you invigilate, but if a student is making this rather hard for you, it's worth remembering that they may be dealing with difficult circumstances in their personal lives.

Invigilators, like all other school or college staff, have a responsibility for young people's care, safety and well-being. Your safeguarding training will help you to know how to respond if a young person confides in you, and the procedures for passing on any concerns about a student's welfare to your school or college's safeguarding officer. This could include passing on concerns about inappropriate behaviour from a fellow invigilator or member of school staff.

Equal opportunities

Your exam centre will have a policy on inclusion and equal opportunities. The precise wording may differ, but the key point is that it is unlawful to discriminate against students on the grounds of disability, race or gender.

In practice, this will involve both formal access arrangements and general care for someone with a disability in the exam hall. For example, where a dyslexic candidate who gets granted extra time under access arrangements is still working, invigilators could make sure they are very quiet when clearing up after the exam.

Invigilators also need to be careful to treat all students equally, and not be influenced by general assumptions about the types of student who misbehave, or try to cheat, or who are bound to be good and work hard.

When working as a team of invigilators, it is useful if the different roles are spread across both sexes, so that either male or female invigilators can cope on their own if necessary.

Invigilation, exams and social media

Whether or not you yourself are an avid user of social media, it's important to know how it impacts on exams.

Awarding bodies monitor social media and websites to pick up comments about copying, collusion, cheating and communication during exams. Candidates mention exam room incidents on social media – even if they shouldn't. Invigilators therefore need to be doubly sure that they have recorded and reported all incidents of malpractice or maladministration through the correct channels.

Centre rules about confidentiality, use of ICT and social media apply to external invigilators as much as to permanent staff. That means no befriending exam candidates online, and no using social media to comment about individual candidates, the behaviour of a group of candidates or your fellow invigilators. Those supposedly private posts, tweets, photos etc. can easily spread to wider networks. Remember that your off-duty social media presence could impact on your invigilator role, and the golden rule is: if in doubt, don't post.

And finally …

The key point is that invigilators keep developing their skills. Invigilating exams is an important, responsible job, and as we've shown, the way invigilators approach it can make all the difference to students' experience of taking exams. We hope that the behaviour management strategies and good practice identified in this booklet will help you to find it a satisfying and enjoyable role.

Happy invigilating!

GLOSSARY

Access arrangements: arrangements provided for candidates with disabilities to enable them to access the exam.

Awarding body: the organisation which sets exams, sometimes called awarding organisation or exam board.

Clash: where arrangements are made for a candidate with two or more exams scheduled at the same time, often involving an invigilator supervising them between exams.

Exam officer: The person responsible for the delivery of exams in the centre. May also be known as the exam manager.

ICE booklet: Instructions for Conducting Examinations. Produced by JCQ in a yellow cover, and also known as the yellow book.

JCQ Joint Council for Qualifications agreed rules for 7 largest awarding organisations in UK: AQA (Assessment and Qualifications Alliance), CCEA (Northern Ireland Council for Curriculum, Examinations and Assessment), City & Guilds, Edexcel, OCR (Oxford Cambridge and RSA Examinations), SQA (Scottish Qualifications Authority) and WJEC (previously Welsh Joint Education Committee).

Orange book: produced by JCQ in an orange cover (previously pink), contains regulations for access arrangements.

Senior or lead invigilator: an experienced invigilator given additional responsibilities. Often in charge in the exam room.

Whistleblowing For what to do in the rare event that the exam office or senior management fail to deal with alleged malpractice see http://www.jcq.org.uk/exams-office/malpractice/public-interest-disclosure-act-whistleblowing. Find JCQ's *Suspected Malpractice in Examinations and Assessments* on their website http://www.jcq.org.uk

ABOUT THE AUTHORS

Anne Borrowdale: A Lead Invigilator who has been invigilating exams since 2005, her experience ranges from large comprehensive schools to international schools and supervising Qualified Lawyers Transfer Tests. In addition, Anne is a trainer, writer and work consultant. **www.anneborrowdale.co.uk**

Barbara Wynn's work in education extends over 38 years: from social priority schools in inner London to 14 years as a headteacher in West Berkshire. Since her retirement she has been involved in a wide range of consultancy work, with a particular focus on student behaviour, restorative approaches and school leadership. Barbara is also a trainer, writer and personal performance coach.

Barbara and Anne set up Exam Team Development to support and develop invigilators and exam office staff. ETD runs a range of enjoyable, active training sessions on the skills described in this book as well as general and senior invigilator training.

This includes training for the Industry Qualifications invigilation awards which ETD developed with the Examination Officers' Association. These awards for standard invigilation, senior invigilation and management of invigilation require study of an online course, an online test, and workplace assessment of knowledge and practical skills. www.examofficers.org.uk has more information.

See **www.examteamdevelopment.co.uk** to learn more about ETD training, and subscribe to ETD's newsletter for details of new courses and special offers. email info@examteamdevelopment.co.uk. You can also find Exam Team Development on Facebook and follow **@ExamTD** on Twitter.